MARKS OF FAITH

DAILY JOURNAL

CREATED BY
ALEXANDRIA JOSEY

Marks of Faith—Copyright ©2023 by Alexandria Josey

Published by UNITED HOUSE Publishing
All rights reserved. No portion of this book may be reproduced or shared in any form—electronic, printed, photocopied, recorded, or by any information storage and retrieval system, without prior written permission from the publisher. The use of short quotations is permitted.

Scripture marked (KJV) are taken from The Authorized (King James) Version. Rights in the Authorized Version in the United Kingdom are vested in the Crown. Reproduced by permission of the Crown's patentee, Cambridge University Press

ISBN: 978-1-952840-31-9
UNITED HOUSE Publishing
Clarkston, Michigan
info@unitedhousepublishing.com
www.unitedhousepublishing.com

Cover and interior layout: Talitha McGuinness, United House Publishing
Printed in the United States of America

2023—First Edition
SPECIAL SALES
Most UNITED HOUSE books are available at special quantity discounts when purchased in bulk by corporations, organizations, and special-interest groups. For information, please e-mail orders@unitedhousepublishing.com.

"I remember falling asleep in church and feeling guilty. I wanted to be there but just sitting and listening was doing nothing for my soul spiritually."

One day, I picked up a notebook I had with me and began writing down parts of the message. Whatever scriptures my Pastor said, whatever phrases he repeated or emphasized, I wrote it all down. I later went back and began to color code different pieces of my writing based on connections I found. The result? A one (sometimes two) page "spark notes" version of the sermon from that Sunday. I started to share the notes with those around me and watched them become inspired. I would often get questions like, "How do you know what to write?", "How can you organize it so neatly while you're listening?", and "Can you share your notes with me?" I started to think the idea of taking notes was not new, but somehow, people struggled to do so. After talking to different people, I realized the biggest issue was organization. They did not know how to organize what they were hearing or even where to start, and that prevented them from being consistent with taking their own notes.

Everyone wants to become better. We make resolutions every year. Sometimes we stick with them for a few days, maybe a few months, but we rarely make a huge lifestyle change. When we aim to become healthier, we change our lifestyles. When we aim to get better at a specific task, we dedicate time and energy to it. If we want to learn more, we take it upon ourselves to study and find resources that help us. If it is so easy in the natural world, shouldn't we do the same to strengthen our spirits? Writing down our interactions with the Word holds us accountable. It allows us to reflect on what we have received and gives us an opportunity to document our walk with Christ.

I took it upon myself to create a tool that would help my brothers and sisters in Christ take meaningful notes they receive from the Word. I launched a small notebook where it had templates, but I knew people needed more direction and guidance. So now, here we are with a journal that provides space for you to pray, space for you to apply, and space to reflect your own journey in His Word.

APPLICATION SECTION
It does not benefit the body of Christ for one person to get fat off the Word but not share it with others so they are also fed. As followers of Christ, we must apply what we hear. We must share what we hear. We do not have to convince others God is real when we show them the Holy Ghost within us through our actions.

- How can I apply this message to my life this week?
- Who or what do I want to impact by my actions this week?

REFLECTION SECTION
Reflecting is part of the spiritual process. When we go through tests and trials, it is important to remember what God has brought you through so you can have hope that He will also bring you through the next battle.

- Where did I apply this message in my life this week?
- Can I connect this to another message I have heard before?

QUARTER 1

It is time to set the bar high and aspire to reach out of your comfort zone. Whether it is the beginning of a new year or just the beginning of you taking your spiritual journey to a new level, it is time to plan and set goals and visions for yourself. The Bible says,

> *"For as the body without the spirit is dead, so faith without works is dead also"*
> *(James 2:26, KJV).*

Let's see God work in our lives while doing our part too. What is our part? It is our responsibility to get into His Word, to apply His Word to our lives, and to be a witness to others of His goodness through the way we live our lives. We see it all of the time—people are so excited to start something new but fail to be consistent because they didn't have something to hold them accountable. It can be uncomfortable being held accountable because if we do not meet our goals, there is something to remind us to get back on track. Discomfort in Him is okay; embrace it. Growth in Him can stretch us, challenge us, and make us confront parts of ourselves that we may try to hide. What parts of you are you willing to expose and let go? As you start writing in this journal, I challenge you to commit to the uncomfortable. So, go into this experience willing to learn, willing to break old habits and start new ones, willing to see connections between His word and your life, willing to listen to what He says about you, and willing to document what is happening in your life. In the end, you will have a tangible testimony that shows your growth on this journey.

Dear God,
Lead me in this journey, and let your Word permeate my heart. I ask you to open my eyes, ears, and heart to receive what You have for me. I have made mistakes and know I am flawed, but You still love me. You see me for who You have called me to be, and it's Your mercy and love that keeps me. I know I need you and I need your Word in my life to guide me. I want to grow in You and be more like You. Let my efforts be seen by You, and let Your will be done in my life. I know I need You, and I know life with You is better than life without You. Give me the strength to be disciplined in this new path I am about to take with You. Give me the confidence to trust Your process. In Jesus' name, Amen.

GOALS TARGETED:

_____

_____

_____

Week 1 - Personal Notes/Prayer
Date: _____

Reference Scriptures

Personal Notes/Prayer

Week 1 - Sermon Notes

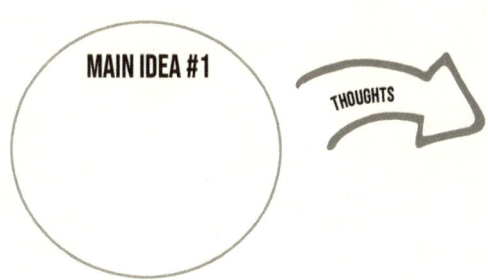

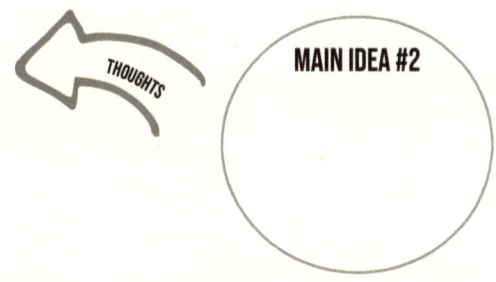

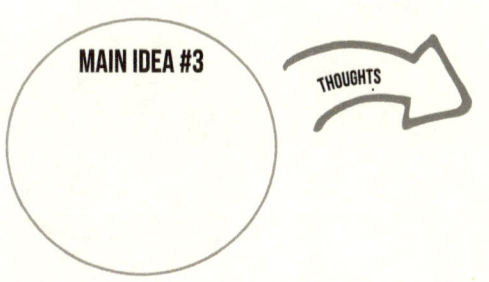

How am I going to apply this to my life this week?

End of the week reflection.
Did I actually apply the message? What was the impact on myself and others?

Week 2 - Personal Notes/Prayer
Date: _____

Reference Scriptures

Personal Notes/Prayer

Week 2 - Sermon Notes

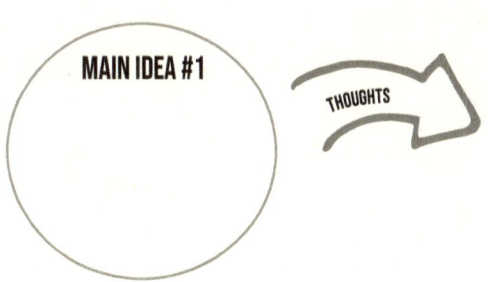

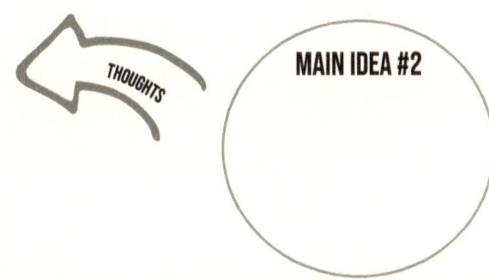

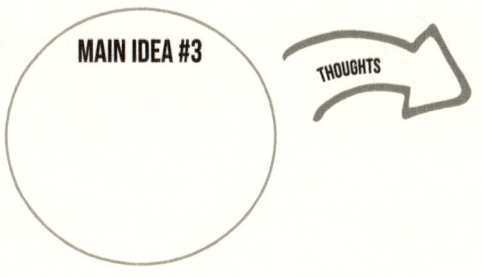

How am I going to apply this to my life this week?

End of the week reflection.
Did I actually apply the message? What was the impact on myself and others?

Week 3 - Personal Notes/Prayer
Date: _____

Reference Scriptures

Personal Notes/Prayer

Week 3 - Sermon Notes

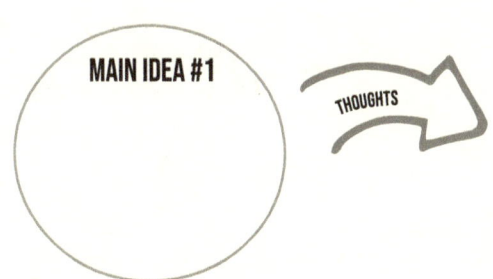

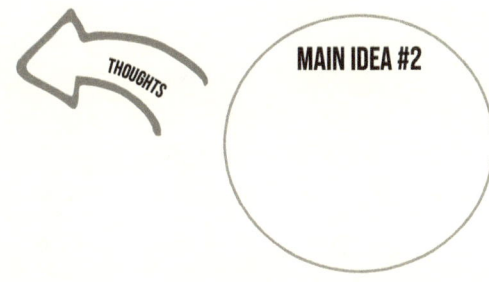

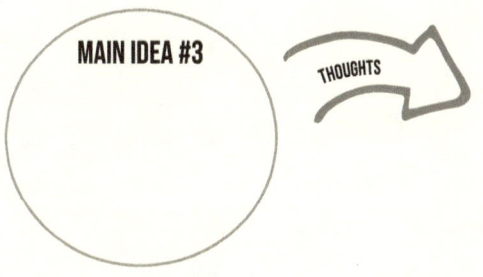

How am I going to apply this to my life this week?

End of the week reflection.
Did I actually apply the message? What was the impact on myself and others?

Week 4 - Personal Notes/Prayer
Date: _____

Reference Scriptures

Personal Notes/Prayer

Week 4 - Sermon Notes

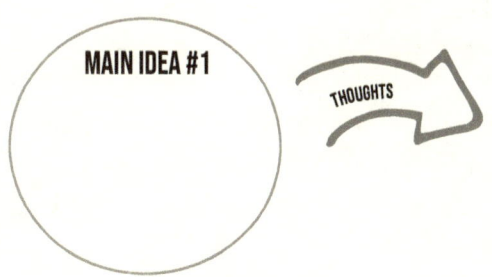

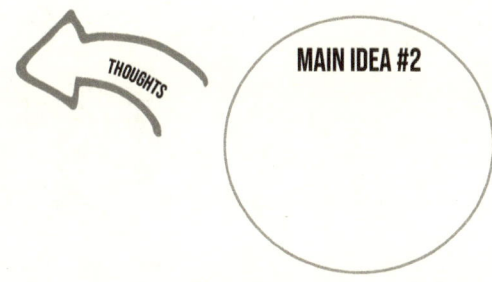

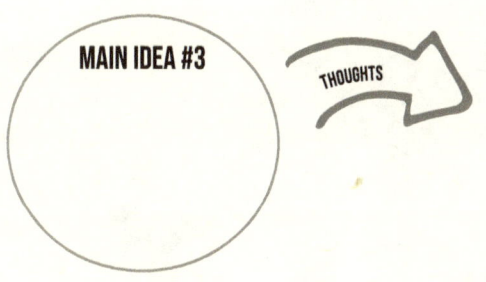

How am I going to apply this to my life this week?

End of the week reflection.
Did I actually apply the message? What was the impact on myself and others?

Week 5 - Personal Notes/Prayer
Date: _____

Reference Scriptures

Personal Notes/Prayer

Week 5 - Sermon Notes

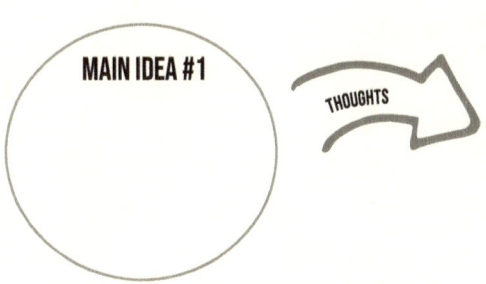

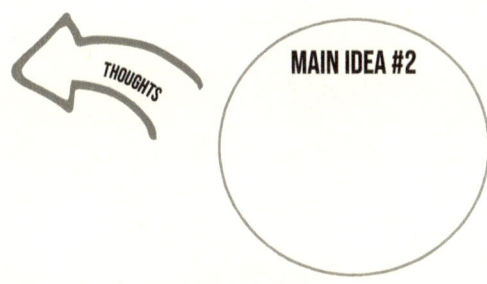

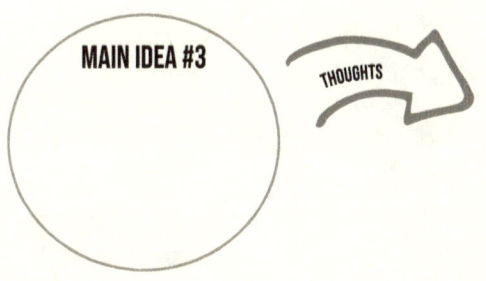

How am I going to apply this to my life this week?

End of the week reflection.
Did I actually apply the message? What was the impact on myself and others?

Week 6 - Personal Notes/Prayer
Date: _____

Reference Scriptures

Personal Notes/Prayer

Week 6 - Sermon Notes

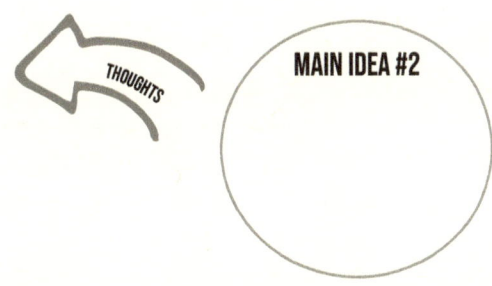

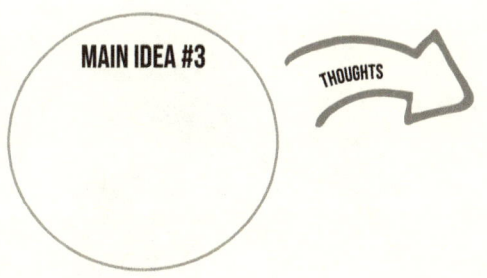

How am I going to apply this to my life this week?

End of the week reflection.
Did I actually apply the message? What was the impact on myself and others?

Week 7 - Personal Notes/Prayer
Date: _____

Reference Scriptures

Personal Notes/Prayer

Week 7 - Sermon Notes

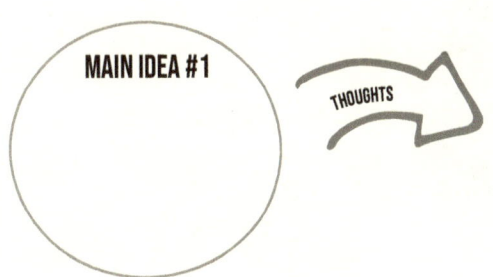

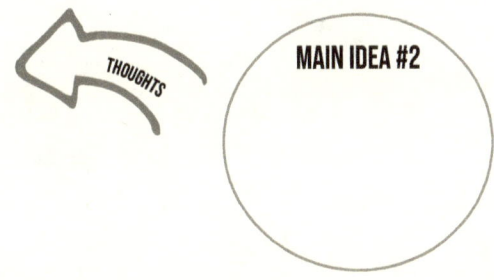

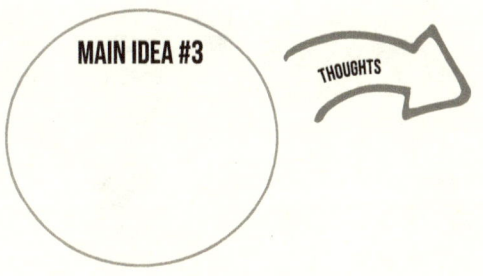

How am I going to apply this to my life this week?

End of the week reflection.
Did I actually apply the message? What was the impact on myself and others?

Week 8 - Personal Notes/Prayer
Date: _____

Reference Scriptures

Personal Notes/Prayer

Week 8 - Sermon Notes

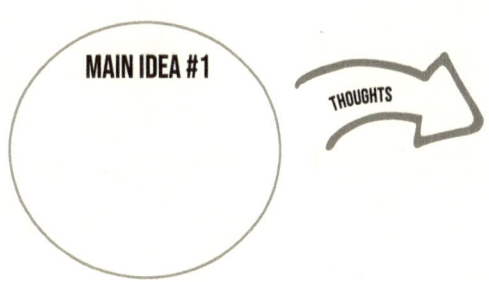

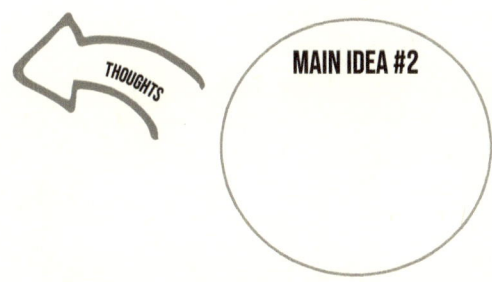

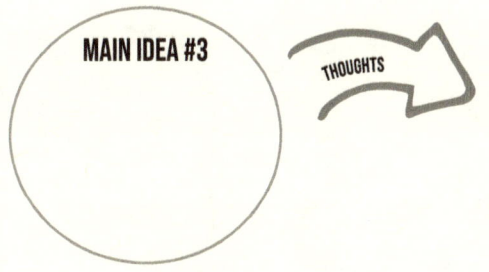

How am I going to apply this to my life this week?

End of the week reflection.
Did I actually apply the message? What was the impact on myself and others?

Week 9 - Personal Notes/Prayer
Date: _____

Reference Scriptures

Personal Notes/Prayer

Week 9 - Sermon Notes

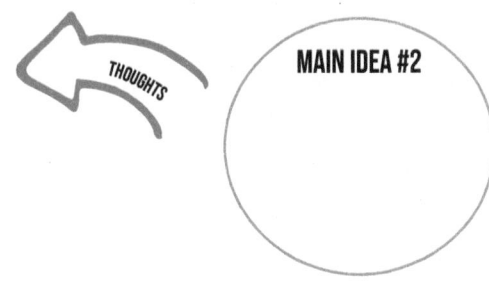

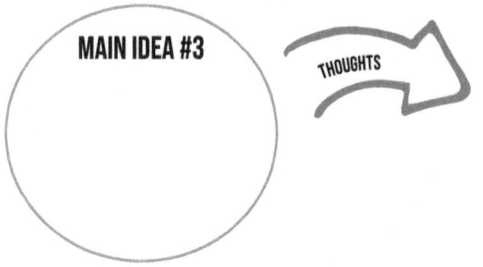

How am I going to apply this to my life this week?

End of the week reflection.
Did I actually apply the message? What was the impact on myself and others?

Week 10 - Personal Notes/Prayer
Date: _____

Reference Scriptures

Personal Notes/Prayer

Week 10 - Sermon Notes

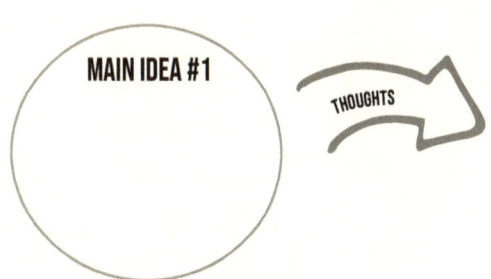

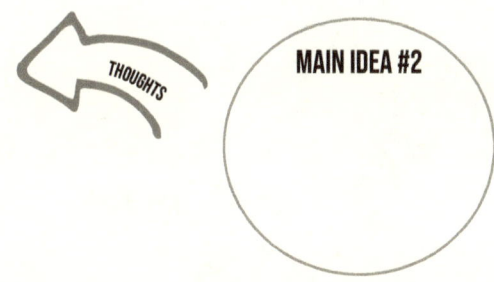

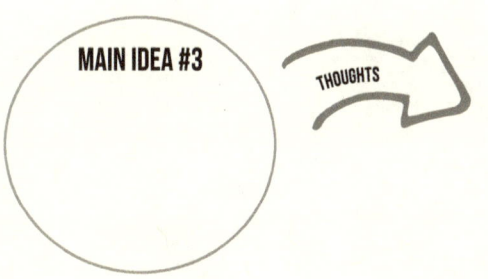

How am I going to apply this to my life this week?

End of the week reflection.
Did I actually apply the message? What was the impact on myself and others?

Week 11 - Personal Notes/Prayer
Date: _____

Reference Scriptures

Personal Notes/Prayer

Week 11 - Sermon Notes

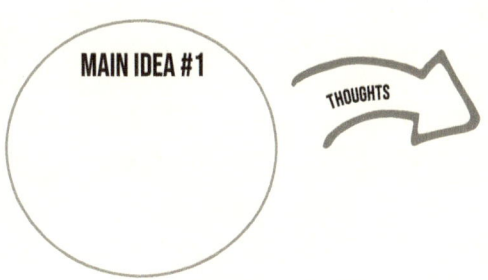

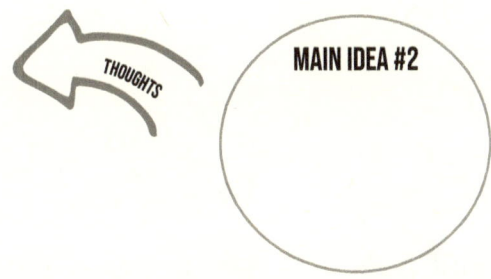

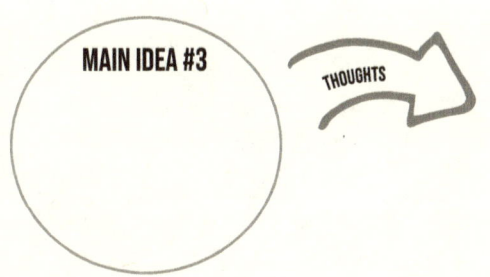

How am I going to apply this to my life this week?

End of the week reflection.
Did I actually apply the message? What was the impact on myself and others?

Week 12 - Personal Notes/Prayer
Date: _____

Reference Scriptures

Personal Notes/Prayer

Week 12 - Sermon Notes

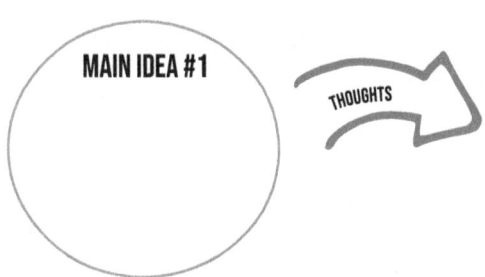

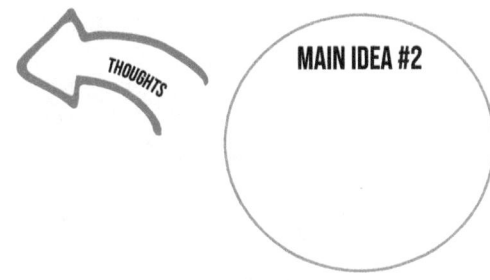

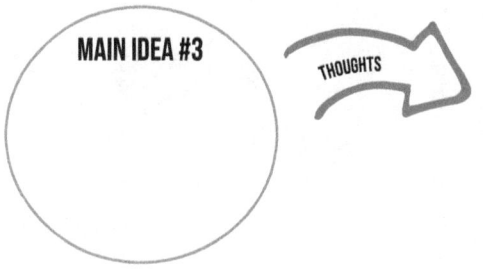

How am I going to apply this to my life this week?

End of the week reflection.
Did I actually apply the message? What was the impact on myself and others?

Week 13 - Personal Notes/Prayer
Date: _____

Reference Scriptures

Personal Notes/Prayer

Week 13 - Sermon Notes

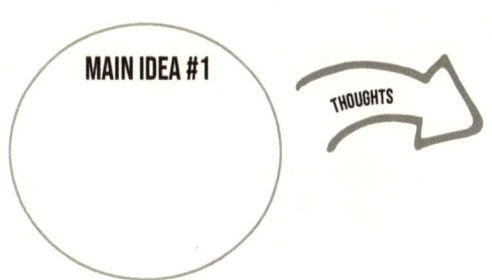

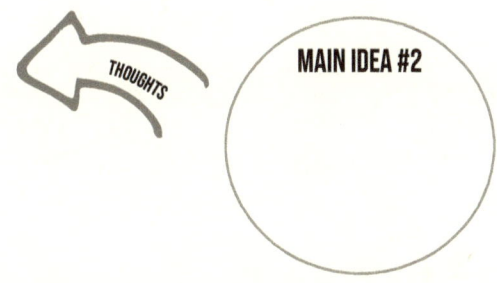

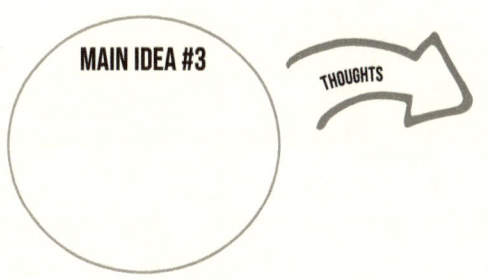

How am I going to apply this to my life this week?

End of the week reflection.
Did I actually apply the message? What was the impact on myself and others?

QUARTER 2

You have made it one-quarter of the way through your journal! How does it feel? Take a few moments to reflect and look back on what you have written. Were there entries that you felt God was flowing through you and onto the page? Were there days where all you could write was "Dear God" and nothing else? This is a process, and as you ebb and flow through it, know that you are not alone. As a believer, you are part of a community: the Kingdom of God. Don't be ashamed or afraid to reach out to others and ask for help. Sharing your stories, testimonies, and connections might be the very thing that your brother or sister needs to hear to keep them going another day. It can be hard trying to become what God has called you to be without others to encourage you along the way. Just as Jesus had his twelve disciples during his days of ministry, we also need people around us who support our goals and understand we are trying to elevate to the next level.

My spiritual father, Bishop Bertram Hinton Jr., once did a Bible Study about the elements of a shift. As we become more invested in who God has called us to be and become more aligned with His word, we will start to see a shift within ourselves. As we take away things that do not serve His purpose for us (unfortunately, that can be people at times), we must be mindful of what we are repurposing that space for. For example, many of us have counter spaces, desks, and tables in our homes that we place junk mail and other miscellaneous things on. If you clean off those areas, they become empty and exposed. They can easily become cluttered again, which would lead you back to where you started. However, if you give those areas a purpose, whether it's a plant, an organizer for your mail, picture frames, etc., now those areas are less likely to be a mess. Take that scenario and apply it to your life. When we start to move away from habits, addictions, and lifestyles that don't align with where we are striving to be, we have to replace that void with something else. That something else is the Holy Spirit. We give people, places, and things time and energy, which are valuable. But, those same people, places, and things are not always valuable in return. Often, we can find ourselves focusing on things that end in sorrow and stress. But when you tap into the Holy Spirit, that same time, energy, and even the gifts you possess can now be spent on things that bring you fulfilling joy. I remember entertaining someone who I thought was fulfilling me, but ultimately, I was left feeling exhausted emotionally and spiritually. Time spent on the last heartbreak can now be time spent strengthening your relationship with loved ones and time in His word.

We are human, and it's our nature to want to be connected to others, but we must be diligent about where people and things fall into our lives. This quarter, take time to keep the pace and remain consistent in this journey. If you haven't been consistent, then this is an opportunity for you to shift and make adjustments. Where did you fall short? What was the reason? Address it and find a way to get back on top. Whether you fall short or keep the pace, keep going. The reward in the end is worth it.

Dear God,
I made a commitment to You and myself that I would take this chance to grow deeper in You. There may have been days where I struggled, but I know that struggling with You yields a blessed reward. I want to do better, and I want to become consistent in You. Help me be bold enough to see my flaws and find the lesson learned. Let me use my testimony as inspiration for my brothers and sisters. Let me not be afraid, for I know that You are with me. Take my heart and mind and align it with Your will. I love You, and I know I'm loved by You. Keep me and help me remain faithful to You. In Jesus' name, Amen.

GOALS TARGETED:

_____

_____

_____

Week 14 - Personal Notes/Prayer
Date: _____

Reference Scriptures

Personal Notes/Prayer

Week 14 - Sermon Notes

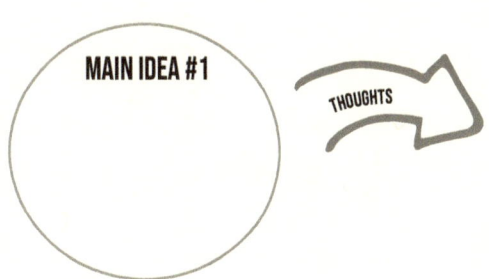

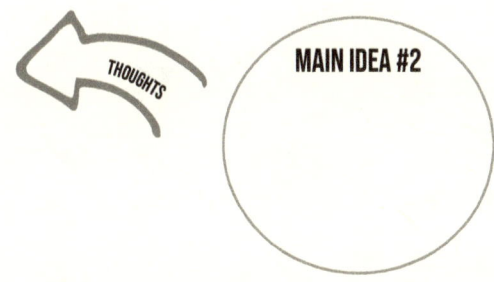

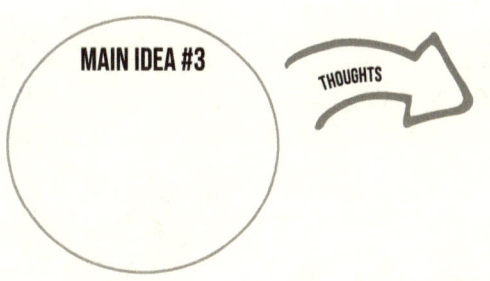

How am I going to apply this to my life this week?

End of the week reflection.
Did I actually apply the message? What was the impact on myself and others?

Week 15 - Personal Notes/Prayer
Date: _____

Reference Scriptures

Personal Notes/Prayer

Week 15 - Sermon Notes

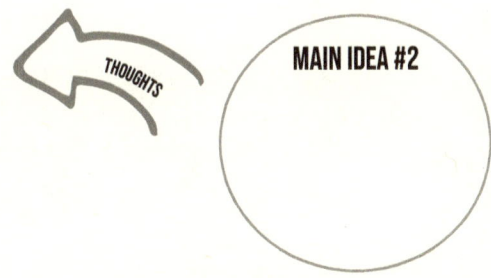

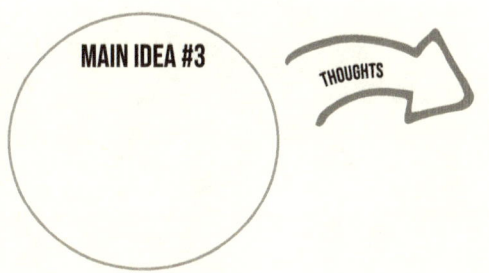

How am I going to apply this to my life this week?

End of the week reflection.
Did I actually apply the message? What was the impact on myself and others?

Week 16 - Personal Notes/Prayer
Date: _____

Reference Scriptures

Personal Notes/Prayer

Week 16 - Sermon Notes

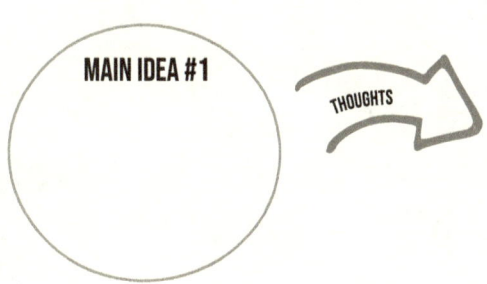

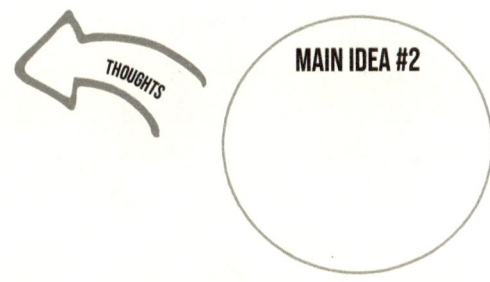

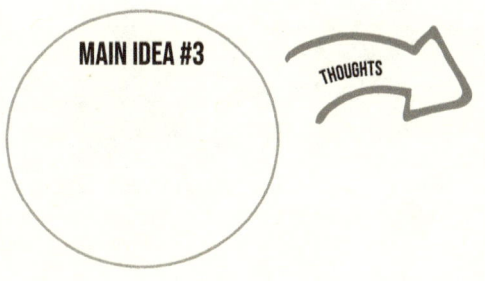

How am I going to apply this to my life this week?

End of the week reflection.
Did I actually apply the message? What was the impact on myself and others?

Week 17 - Personal Notes/Prayer
Date: _____

Reference Scriptures

Personal Notes/Prayer

Week 17 - Sermon Notes

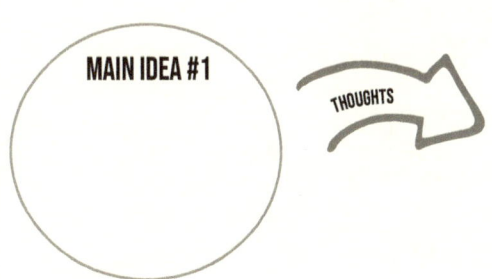

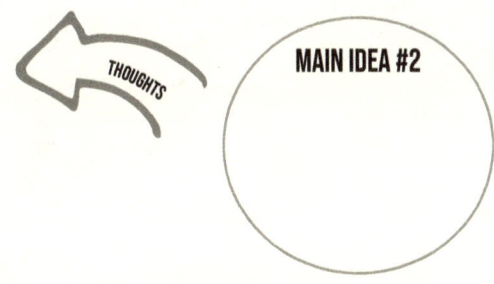

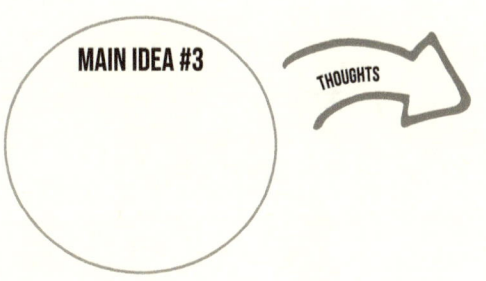

How am I going to apply this to my life this week?

End of the week reflection.
Did I actually apply the message? What was the impact on myself and others?

Week 18 - Personal Notes/Prayer
Date: _____

Reference Scriptures

Personal Notes/Prayer

Week 18 - Sermon Notes

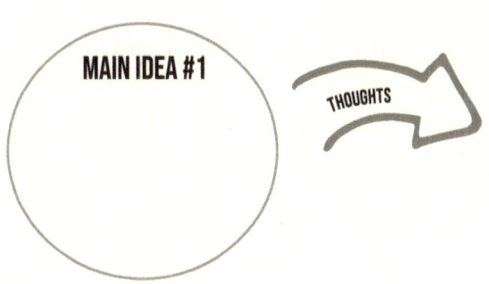

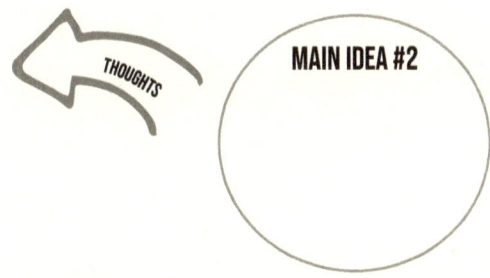

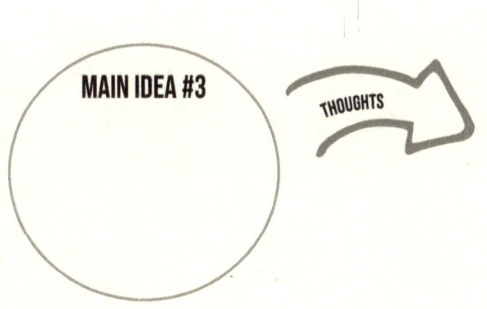

How am I going to apply this to my life this week?

End of the week reflection.
Did I actually apply the message? What was the impact on myself and others?

Week 19 - Personal Notes/Prayer
Date: _____

Reference Scriptures

Personal Notes/Prayer

Week 19 - Sermon Notes

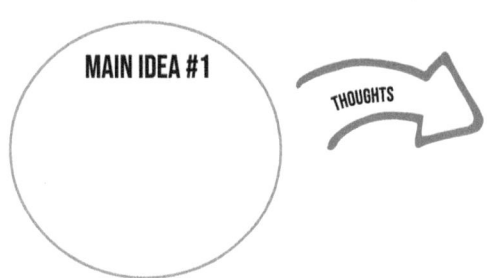

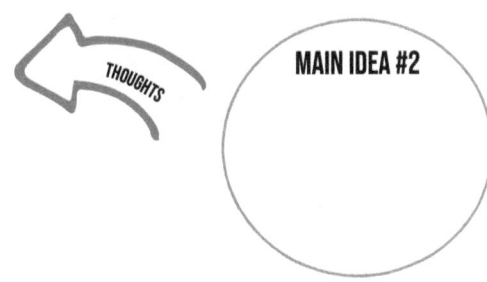

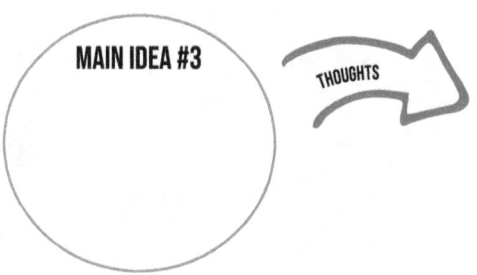

How am I going to apply this to my life this week?

End of the week reflection.
Did I actually apply the message? What was the impact on myself and others?

Week 20 - Personal Notes/Prayer
Date: _____

Reference Scriptures

Personal Notes/Prayer

Week 20 - Sermon Notes

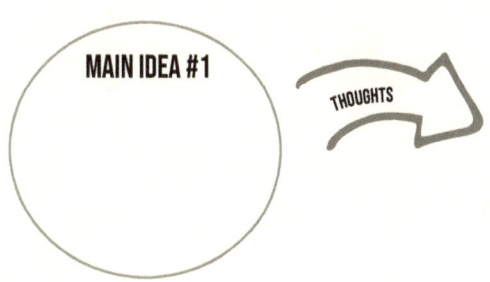

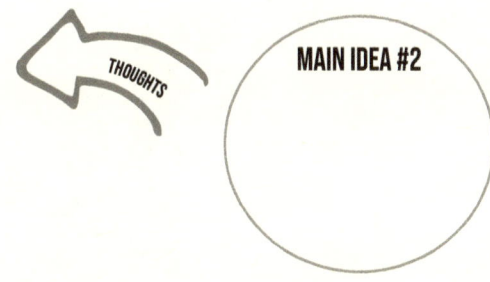

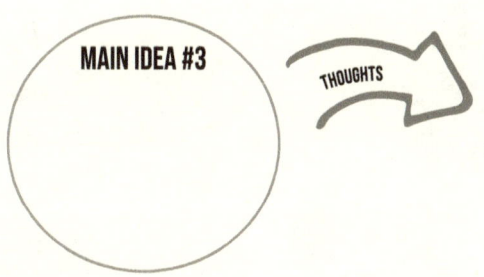

How am I going to apply this to my life this week?

End of the week reflection.
Did I actually apply the message? What was the impact on myself and others?

Week 21 - Personal Notes/Prayer
Date: _____

Reference Scriptures

Personal Notes/Prayer

Week 21 - Sermon Notes

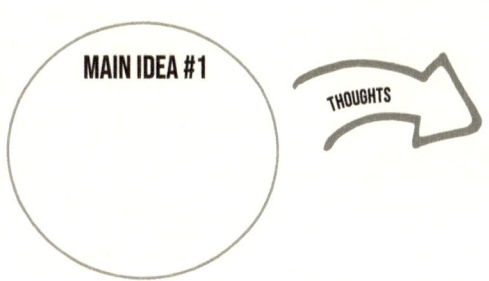

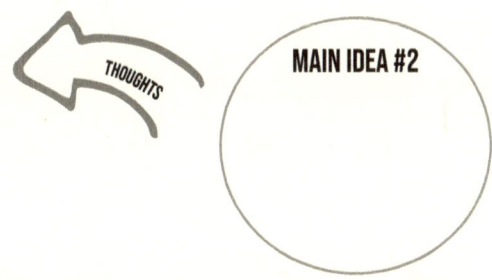

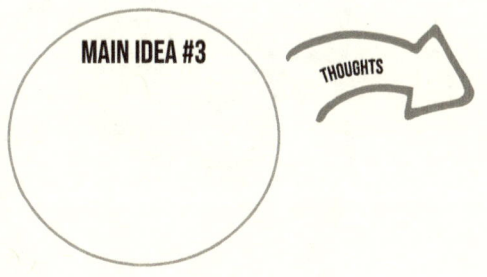

How am I going to apply this to my life this week?

End of the week reflection.
Did I actually apply the message? What was the impact on myself and others?

Week 22 - Personal Notes/Prayer
Date: _____

Reference Scriptures

Personal Notes/Prayer

Week 22 - Sermon Notes

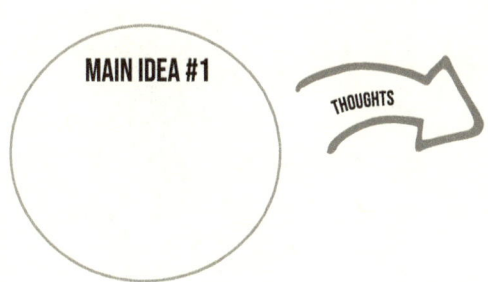

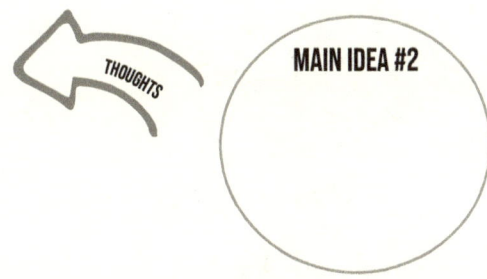

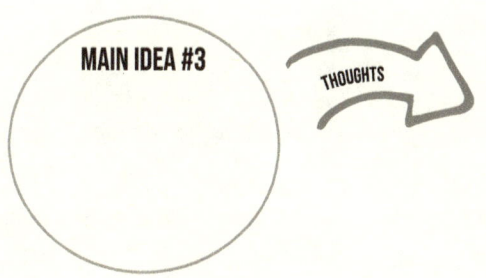

How am I going to apply this to my life this week?

End of the week reflection.
Did I actually apply the message? What was the impact on myself and others?

Week 23 - Personal Notes/Prayer
Date: _____

Reference Scriptures

Personal Notes/Prayer

Week 23 - Sermon Notes

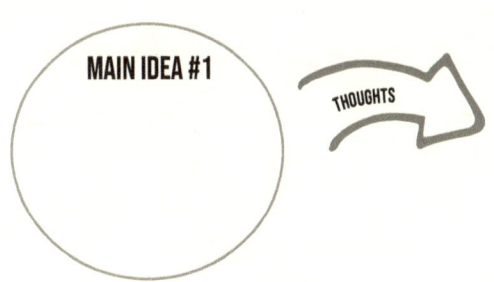

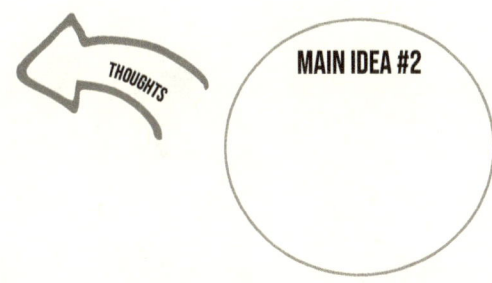

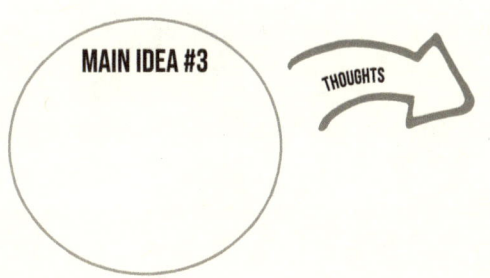

How am I going to apply this to my life this week?

End of the week reflection.
Did I actually apply the message? What was the impact on myself and others?

Week 24 - Personal Notes/Prayer
Date: _____

Reference Scriptures

Personal Notes/Prayer

Week 24 - Sermon Notes

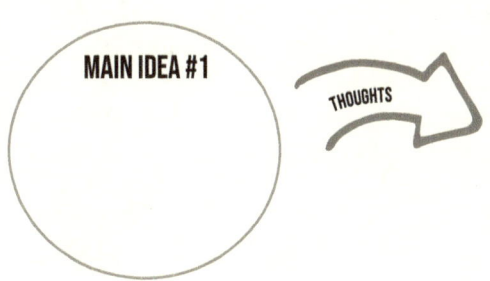

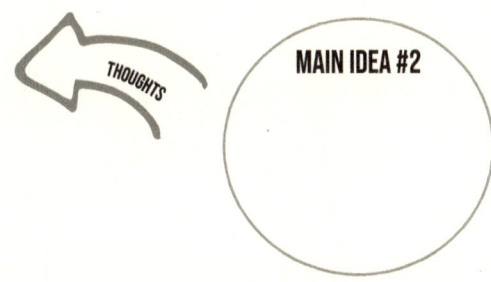

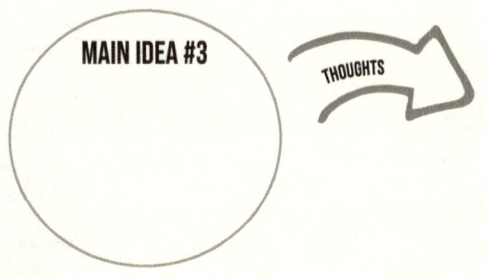

How am I going to apply this to my life this week?

End of the week reflection.
Did I actually apply the message? What was the impact on myself and others?

Week 25 - Personal Notes/Prayer
Date: _____

Reference Scriptures

Personal Notes/Prayer

Week 25 - Sermon Notes

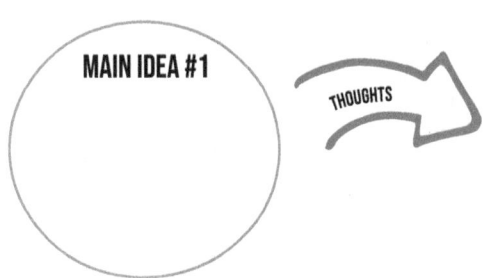

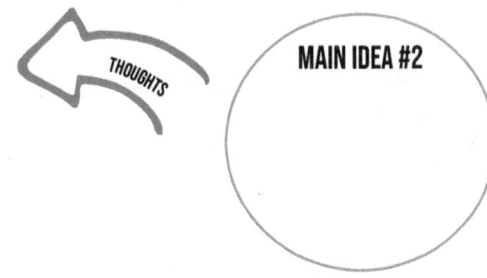

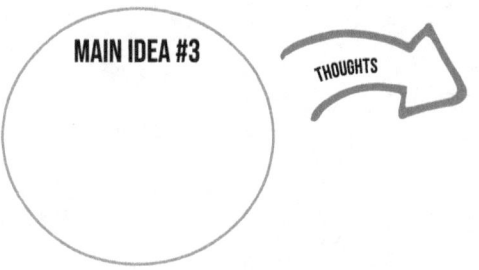

How am I going to apply this to my life this week?

End of the week reflection.
Did I actually apply the message? What was the impact on myself and others?

Week 26 - Personal Notes/Prayer
Date: _____

Reference Scriptures

Personal Notes/Prayer

Week 26 - Sermon Notes

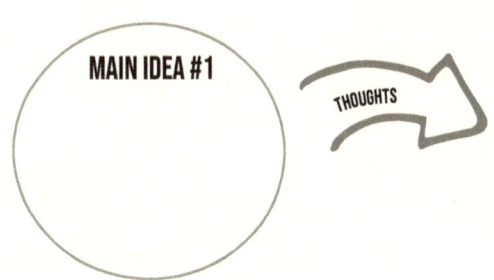

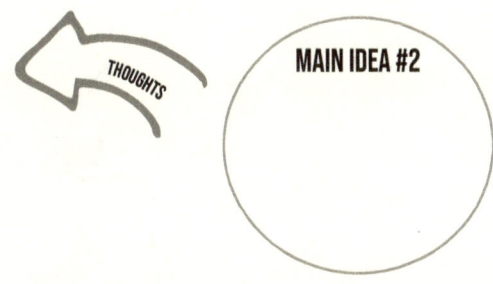

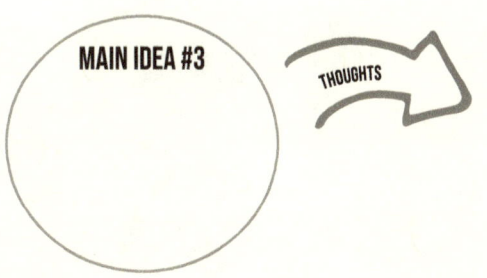

How am I going to apply this to my life this week?

End of the week reflection.
Did I actually apply the message? What was the impact on myself and others?

QUARTER 3

We are at the halfway mark! Six months of diving deeper into His Word, six months of being intentional about connecting God's plan to your life...how do you feel? The halfway mark always reminds me of when I used to run track. I was not a fan of running, but I was decent enough to be on someone's team (sidenote...you may feel at times you're not good enough for something but know that the purpose God set for you is always going to be yours). Anyways, I was a mid-distance runner, and my races were always the 400 meters (one lap around), 800 meters, and the relays associated with those races. Every single time I would get halfway around the track, I always had one of these two thoughts: "Thank you, God, I'm halfway through" or "Dear God, am I really only halfway through?" What determined my mentality was based on how I started the race. If I was controlling my breathing and in a decent place compared to others, I felt good about what was going on. If I was already tired or if I noticed I was behind most runners, then I already felt defeated. Thinking back to those days, I wish someone would have told me that my mindset has an impact on how I perform.

So, how are you running your race? Did you start off strong with intentions? Did you tell yourself early on you would commit no matter what? If so, kudos to you because many people struggle. If you are one of the struggling, I'm telling you it is not too late to change your mindset. You want to grow and get to that next level. You wouldn't have made it this far if you weren't set on it. Even when I didn't have the best mindset during a race, I always finished. Think about the story of Job. He started off at the top and was the leader of the pack in all areas possible. He had everything he could want, and his faith was still tested. Fast forward, Job loses his family, fortune, and health. Now, Job did question God's plan and purpose for his suffering, but he never once actually blamed God. He remained faithful. The Bible says,

> "In all this Job sinned not, nor charged God foolishly"
> (Job 1:22, KJV).

Take a minute or two and ask yourself how you respond to challenges in your life. Do you find yourself blaming others? Do you trust God enough to go through it faithfully? Or is it a mix of both? Go back and look at the goals and intentions you set for yourself when you first began this journey. Reflect on the results of your process thus far. Gain confidence in areas where you have been strengthened, and reset areas where you took a loss. God is still in this journey with you, and you still have room to grow.

Dear God,
You have proven yourself to be faithful time and time again. If you brought me through one struggle, I have no reason to believe you won't

pull me through the next. It's tough being one of Your children because the battles I face are great. I must remain faithful to You even when it looks like the world is against me. I know I'm not alone because I have You. If You are for me, there is no weapon that can prosper against me. You won't let the weapons prosper, but You did say they would form. So, give me the strength and courage to not lose faith in who You've called me to be. Give me the wisdom to hear from You and go in the direction you have paved for me. I made it halfway through because of You, and I know the second half is in Your hands as well. In Jesus' name, I pray, Amen.

GOALS TARGETED:

_____

_____

_____

Week 27 - Personal Notes/Prayer
Date: _____

Reference Scriptures

Personal Notes/Prayer

Week 27 - Sermon Notes

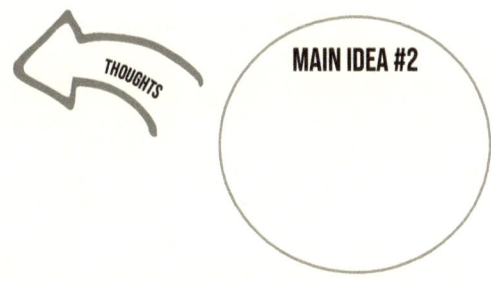

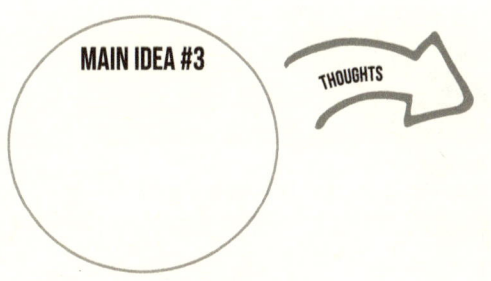

How am I going to apply this to my life this week?

End of the week reflection.
Did I actually apply the message? What was the impact on myself and others?

Week 28 - Personal Notes/Prayer
Date: _____

Reference Scriptures

Personal Notes/Prayer

Week 28 - Sermon Notes

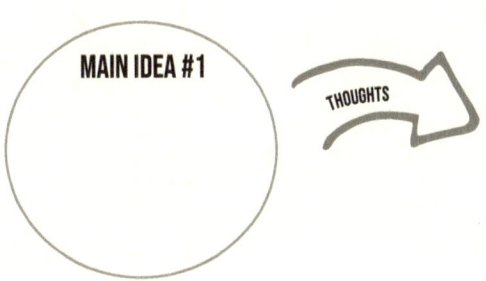

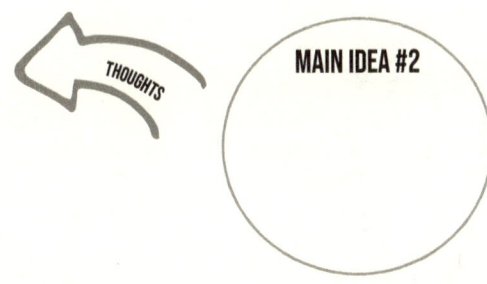

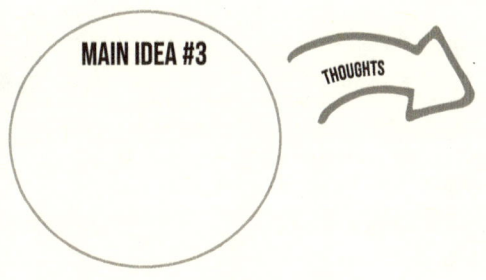

How am I going to apply this to my life this week?

End of the week reflection.
Did I actually apply the message? What was the impact on myself and others?

Week 29 - Personal Notes/Prayer
Date: _____

Reference Scriptures

Personal Notes/Prayer

Week 29 - Sermon Notes

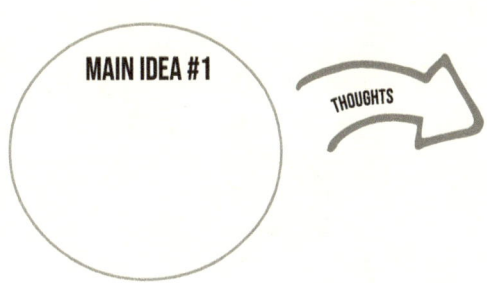

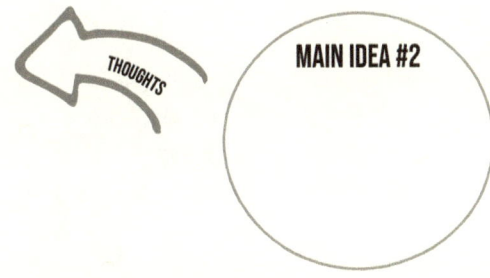

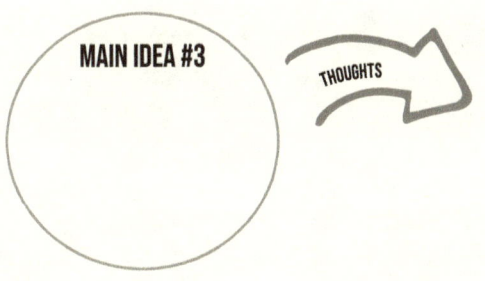

How am I going to apply this to my life this week?

End of the week reflection.
Did I actually apply the message? What was the impact on myself and others?

Week 30 - Personal Notes/Prayer
Date: _____

Reference Scriptures

Personal Notes/Prayer

Week 30 - Sermon Notes

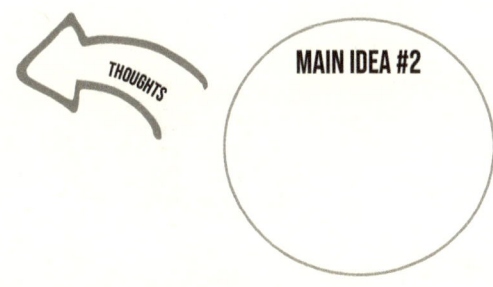

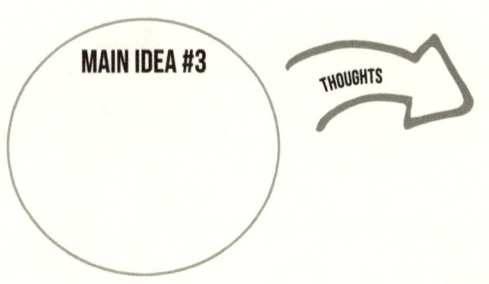

How am I going to apply this to my life this week?

End of the week reflection.
Did I actually apply the message? What was the impact on myself and others?

Week 31 - Personal Notes/Prayer
Date: _____

Reference Scriptures

Personal Notes/Prayer

Week 31 - Sermon Notes

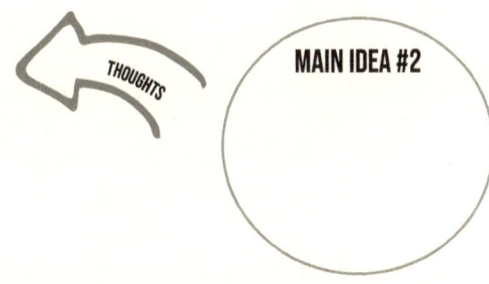

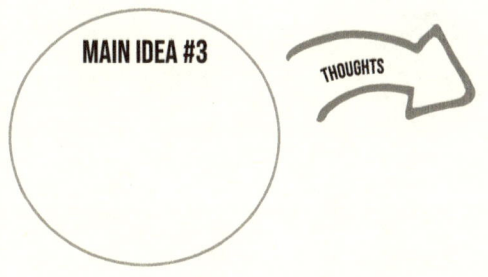

How am I going to apply this to my life this week?

End of the week reflection.
Did I actually apply the message? What was the impact on myself and others?

Week 32 - Personal Notes/Prayer
Date: _____

Reference Scriptures

Personal Notes/Prayer

Week 32 - Sermon Notes

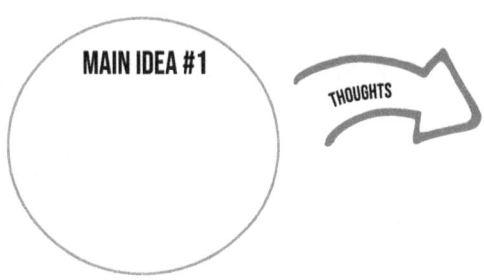

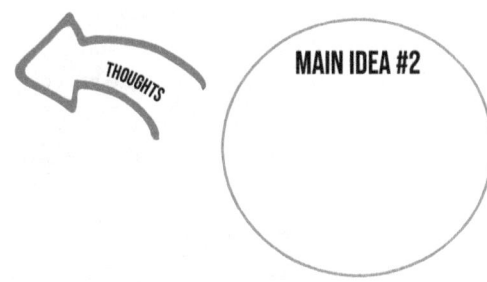

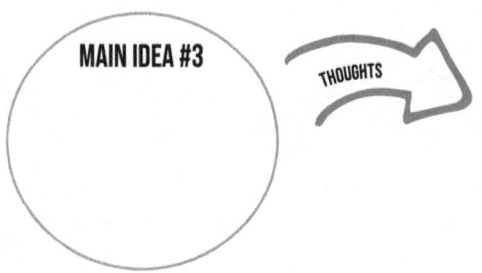

How am I going to apply this to my life this week?

End of the week reflection.
Did I actually apply the message? What was the impact on myself and others?

Week 33 - Personal Notes/Prayer
Date: _____

Reference Scriptures

Personal Notes/Prayer

Week 33 - Sermon Notes

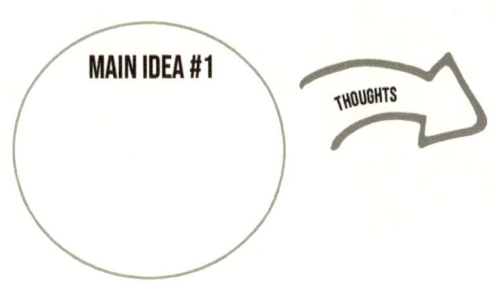

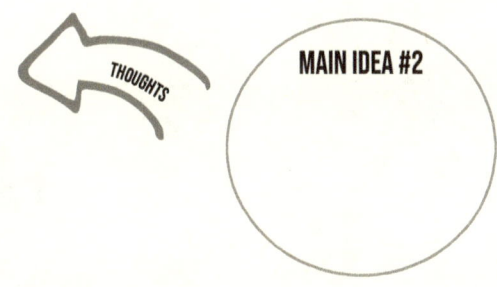

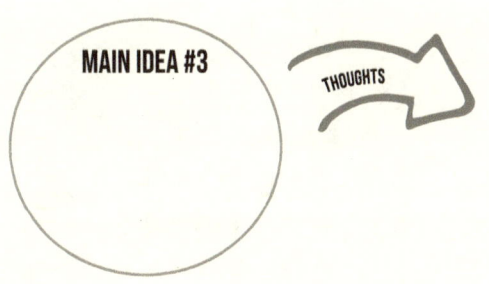

How am I going to apply this to my life this week?

End of the week reflection.
Did I actually apply the message? What was the impact on myself and others?

Week 34 - Personal Notes/Prayer
Date: _____

Reference Scriptures

Personal Notes/Prayer

Week 34 - Sermon Notes

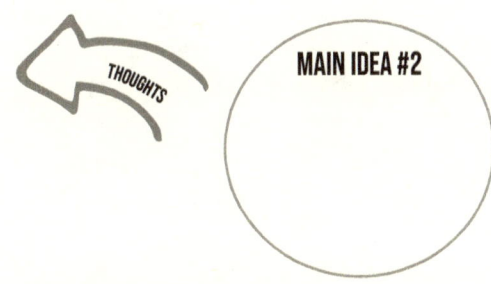

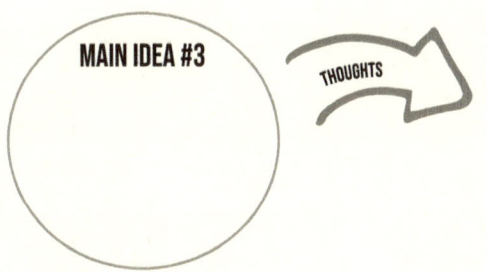

How am I going to apply this to my life this week?

End of the week reflection.
Did I actually apply the message? What was the impact on myself and others?

Week 35 - Personal Notes/Prayer
Date: _____

Reference Scriptures

Personal Notes/Prayer

Week 35 - Sermon Notes

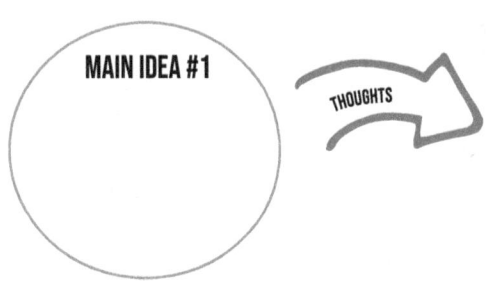

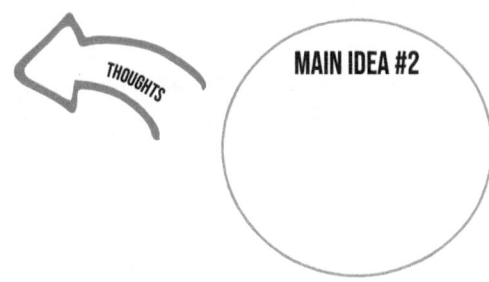

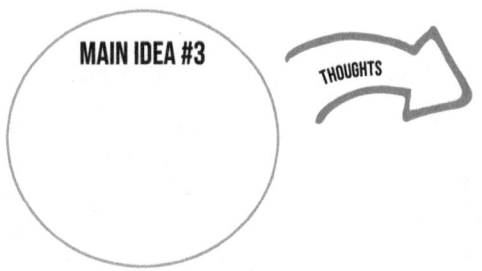

How am I going to apply this to my life this week?

End of the week reflection.
Did I actually apply the message? What was the impact on myself and others?

Week 36 - Personal Notes/Prayer
Date: _____

Reference Scriptures

Personal Notes/Prayer

Week 36 - Sermon Notes

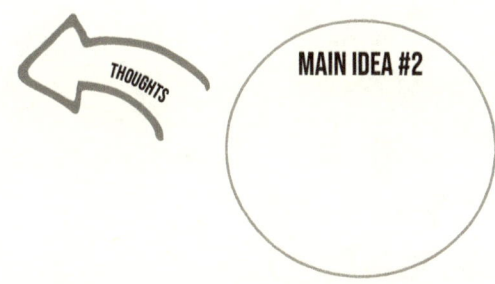

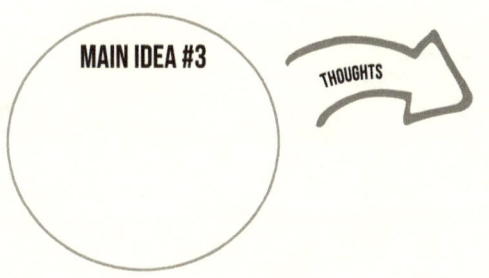

How am I going to apply this to my life this week?

End of the week reflection.
Did I actually apply the message? What was the impact on myself and others?

Week 37 - Personal Notes/Prayer
Date: _____

Reference Scriptures

Personal Notes/Prayer

Week 37 - Sermon Notes

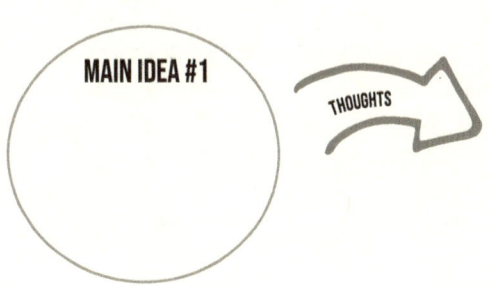

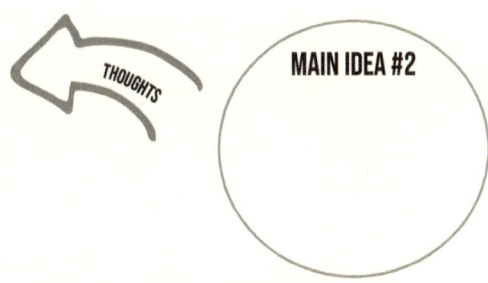

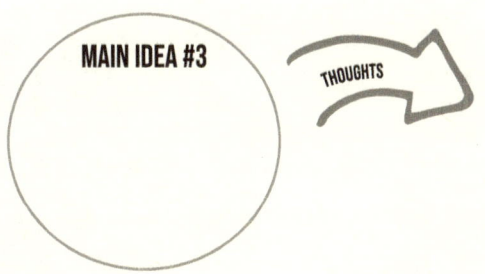

How am I going to apply this to my life this week?

End of the week reflection.
Did I actually apply the message? What was the impact on myself and others?

Week 38 - Personal Notes/Prayer
Date: _____

Reference Scriptures

Personal Notes/Prayer

Week 38 - Sermon Notes

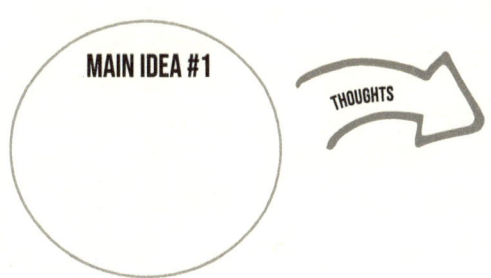

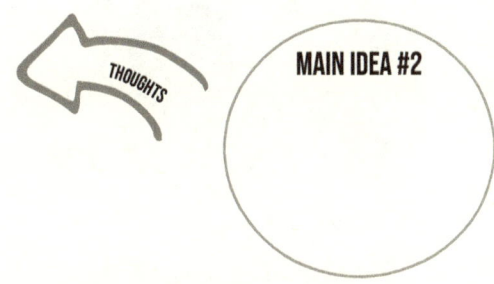

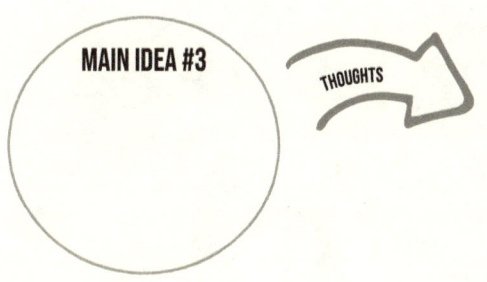

How am I going to apply this to my life this week?

End of the week reflection.
Did I actually apply the message? What was the impact on myself and others?

Week 40 - Personal Notes/Prayer
Date: _____

Reference Scriptures

Personal Notes/Prayer

Week 40 - Sermon Notes

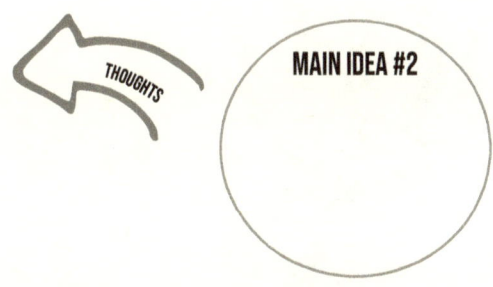

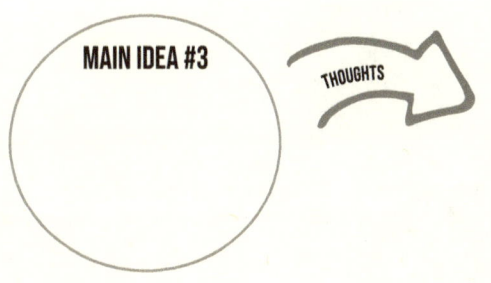

How am I going to apply this to my life this week?

End of the week reflection.
Did I actually apply the message? What was the impact on myself and others?

QUARTER 4

I pray this experience has been life-changing, motivational, and full of intentions that have elevated you to another level in Christ. This is the season to give it your all. If you were holding back before, let your inhibitions go. This experience and journey are yours and what you make of it. God has given us free will, and it's our responsibility to use it for His glory. Some people take that ability and use it to better themselves, others acknowledge it but are unsure how to really use it, and some are unaware that this ability is theirs to call their own. When you first started this journey, you made the choice to become invested in your walk with Christ. You made the choice to push yourself to new heights. You took the risk and opened yourself up to who you are and where you are spiritually. You exposed parts of yourself that may have been hidden, and you let go of things that didn't align with who God called you to be. You found parts of you that God had been pulling and tugging on for some time, and you embraced parts of yourself that have always been aligned with your purpose. No matter how uncomfortable or uneasy it felt, you trusted God through it all with hopes that, in the end, you can say this was all worth it. We are coming close to the end of our journal experience, but that doesn't mean this is the end of your journey. This journal was and is a simple tool for you to become more aligned with His word and see the connections between what He says and the life you live. Whether you've stuck with the plan you set for yourself in the beginning or slipped up a few times along the way, let this quarter be your best quarter yet.

Dear God,
Thank you for allowing me the opportunity to get to grow in You and build a closer relationship with You. Some may question who You are, and others may question who they are in Your eyes. I want to be the one who is confident in who You've called me to be. I am the head and not the tail. I am above and not beneath. I am the lender and not the borrower. I am growing in You every day, and another day is another opportunity for Your will to be done. I am far from perfect, but I know that You are not looking for perfection. You want my best every time I try, and that's what I strive to give You. Even when I fall short, I ask for forgiveness with the hope of your mercy falling on me and Your love embracing me. I am a child of Yours, and I want to say that I made my Father proud. I want to say I'm proud of myself. I want to say that I was able to accomplish and complete a good deed in You. Hold my head high, Father, as I continue to press on, and if I should stumble, I pray that Your hand catches my fall and pushes me forward to the finish line. In Jesus' name, I pray, amen.

GOALS TARGETED:

_____

_____

_____

Week 41 - Personal Notes/Prayer
Date: _____

Reference Scriptures

Personal Notes/Prayer

Week 41 - Sermon Notes

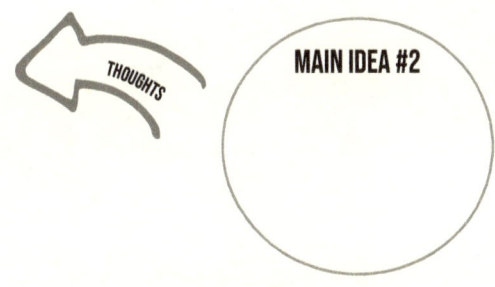

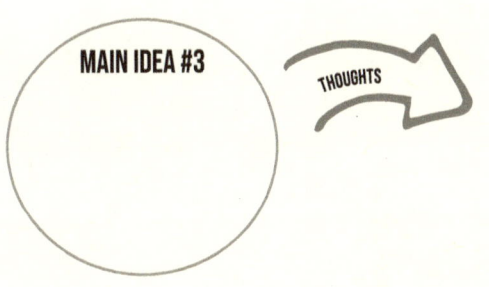

How am I going to apply this to my life this week?

End of the week reflection.
Did I actually apply the message? What was the impact on myself and others?

Week 42 - Personal Notes/Prayer
Date: _____

Reference Scriptures

Personal Notes/Prayer

Week 42 - Sermon Notes

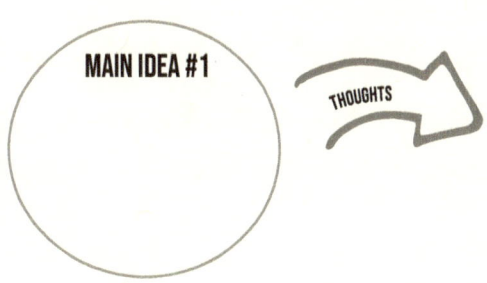

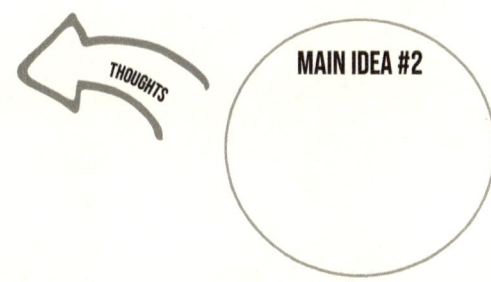

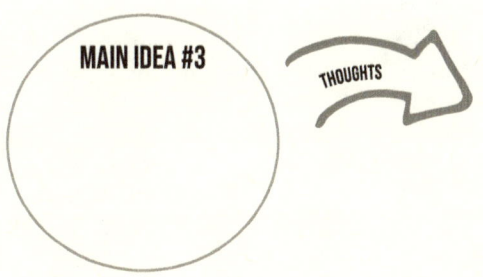

How am I going to apply this to my life this week?

End of the week reflection.
Did I actually apply the message? What was the impact on myself and others?

Week 43 - Personal Notes/Prayer
Date: _____

Reference Scriptures

Personal Notes/Prayer

Week 43 - Sermon Notes

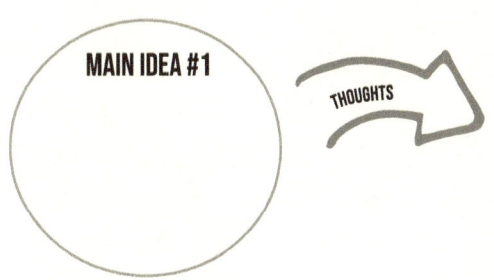

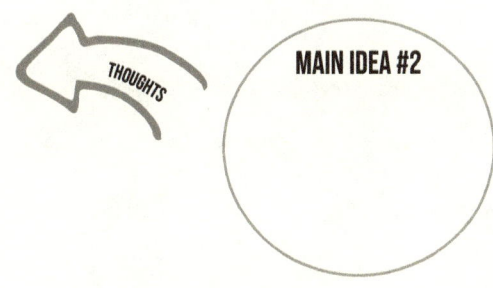

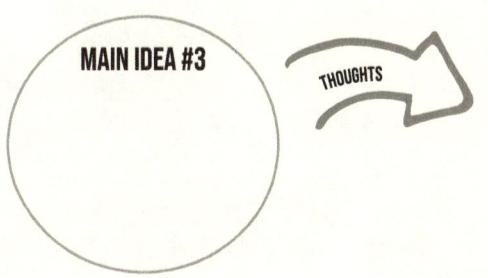

How am I going to apply this to my life this week?

End of the week reflection.
Did I actually apply the message? What was the impact on myself and others?

Week 44 - Personal Notes/Prayer
Date: _____

Reference Scriptures

Personal Notes/Prayer

Week 44 - Sermon Notes

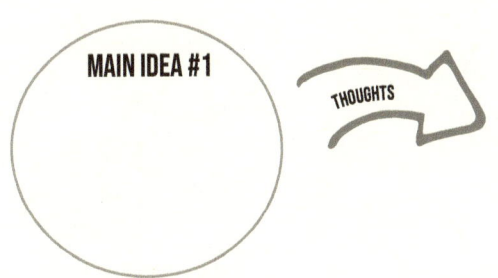

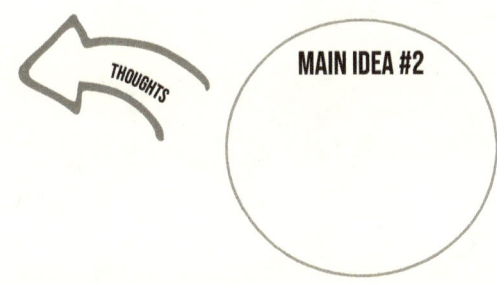

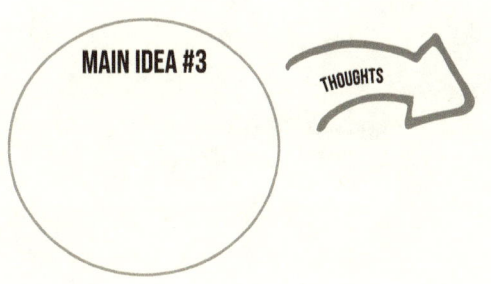

How am I going to apply this to my life this week?

End of the week reflection.
Did I actually apply the message? What was the impact on myself and others?

Week 45 - Personal Notes/Prayer
Date: _____

Reference Scriptures

Personal Notes/Prayer

Week 45 - Sermon Notes

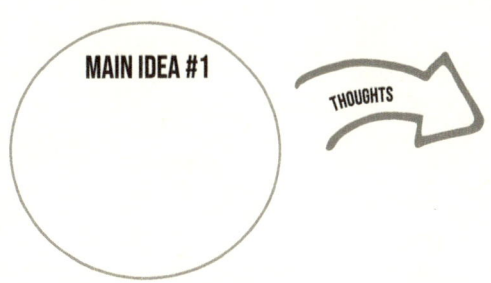

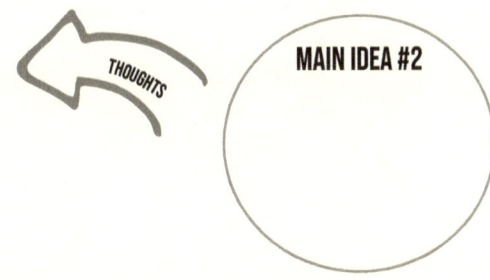

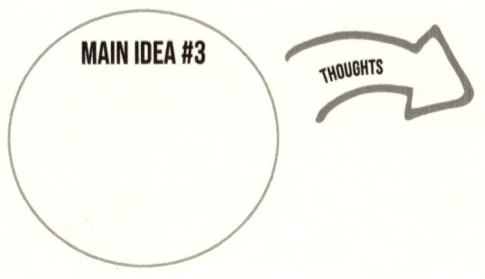

How am I going to apply this to my life this week?

End of the week reflection.
Did I actually apply the message? What was the impact on myself and others?

Week 46 - Personal Notes/Prayer
Date: _____

Reference Scriptures

Personal Notes/Prayer

Week 46 - Sermon Notes

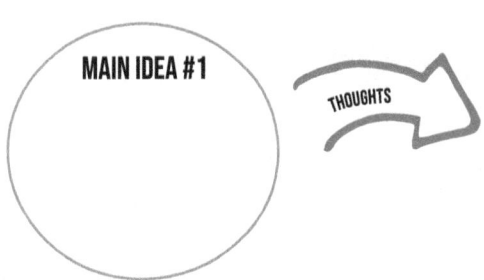

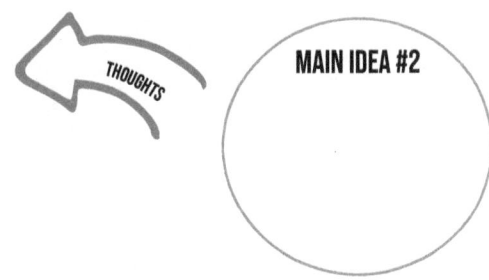

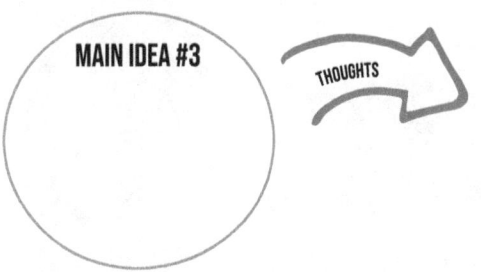

How am I going to apply this to my life this week?

End of the week reflection.
Did I actually apply the message? What was the impact on myself and others?

Week 47 - Personal Notes/Prayer
Date: _____

Reference Scriptures

Personal Notes/Prayer

Week 47 - Sermon Notes

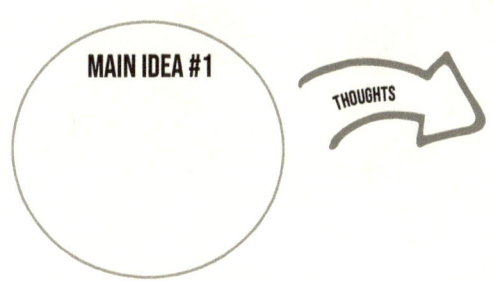

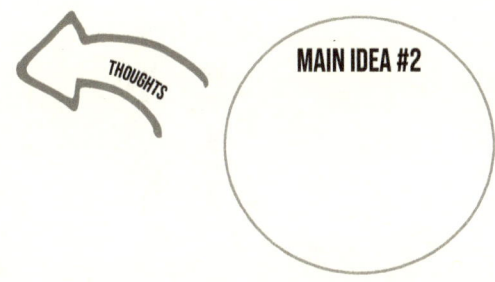

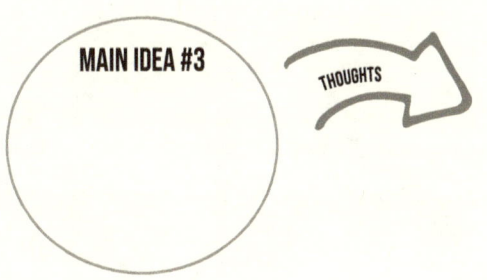

How am I going to apply this to my life this week?

End of the week reflection.
Did I actually apply the message? What was the impact on myself and others?

Week 48 - Personal Notes/Prayer
Date: _____

Reference Scriptures

Personal Notes/Prayer

Week 48 - Sermon Notes

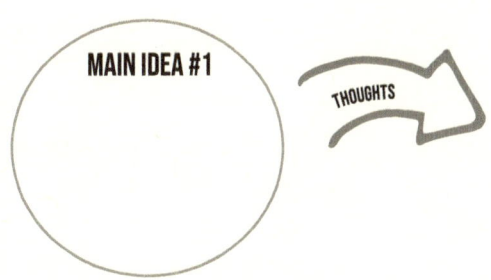

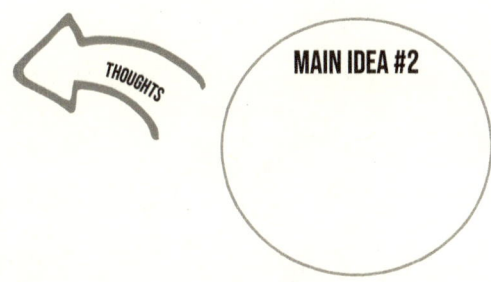

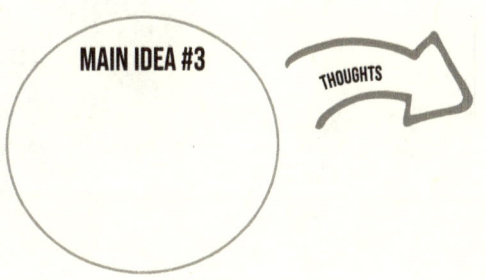

How am I going to apply this to my life this week?

End of the week reflection.
Did I actually apply the message? What was the impact on myself and others?

Week 49 - Personal Notes/Prayer
Date: _____

Reference Scriptures

Personal Notes/Prayer

Week 49 - Sermon Notes

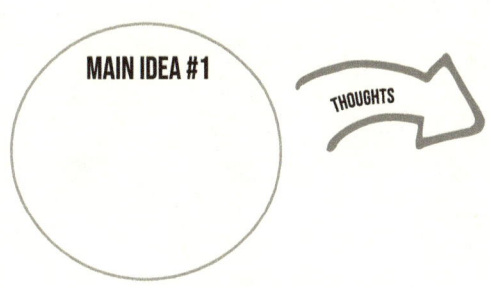

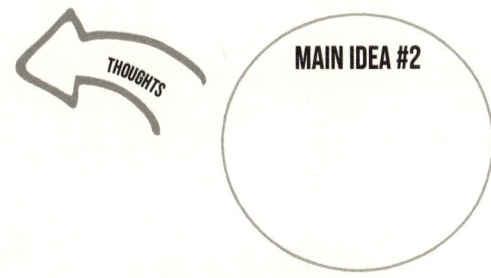

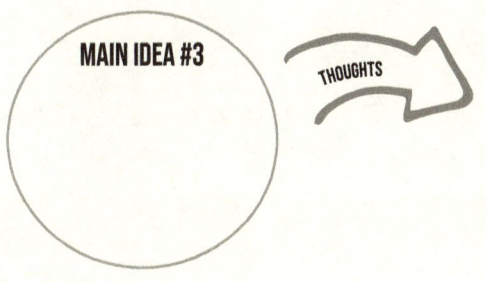

How am I going to apply this to my life this week?

End of the week reflection.
Did I actually apply the message? What was the impact on myself and others?

Week 50 - Personal Notes/Prayer
Date: _____

Reference Scriptures

Personal Notes/Prayer

Week 50 - Sermon Notes

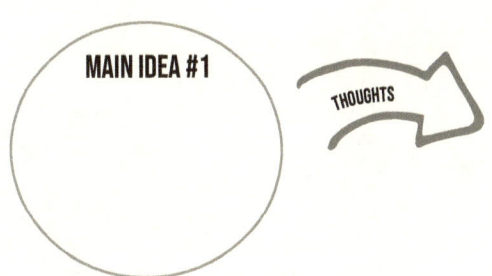

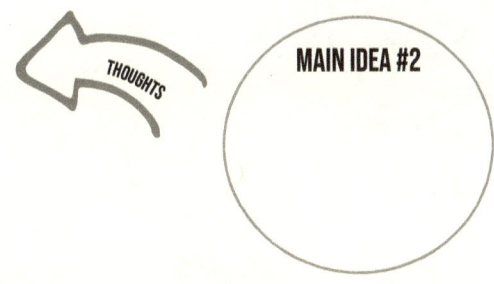

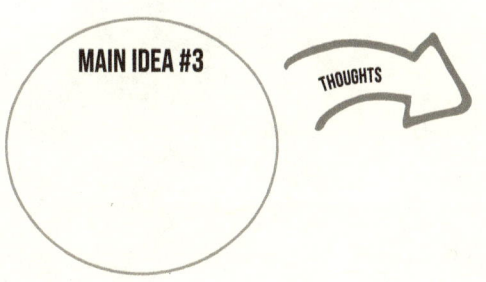

How am I going to apply this to my life this week?

End of the week reflection.
Did I actually apply the message? What was the impact on myself and others?

Week 51 - Personal Notes/Prayer
Date: _____

Reference Scriptures

Personal Notes/Prayer

Week 51 - Sermon Notes

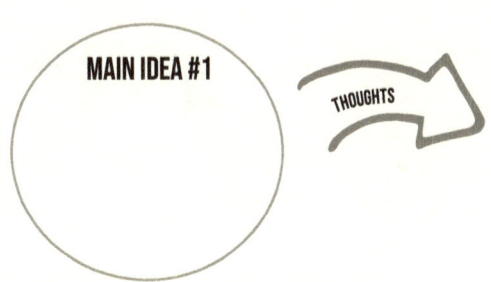

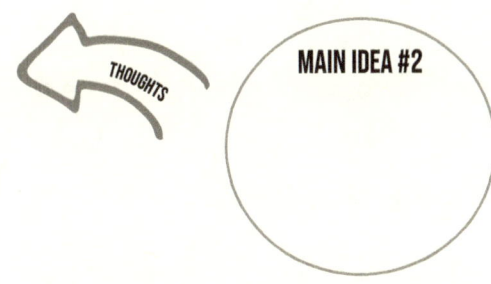

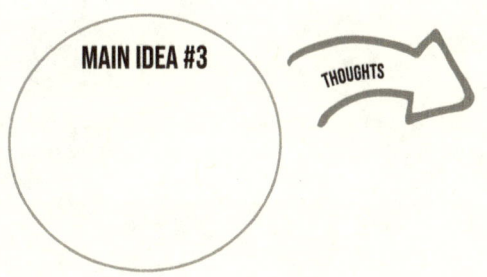

How am I going to apply this to my life this week?

End of the week reflection.
Did I actually apply the message? What was the impact on myself and others?

Week 52 - Personal Notes/Prayer
Date: _____

Reference Scriptures

Personal Notes/Prayer

Week 52 - Sermon Notes

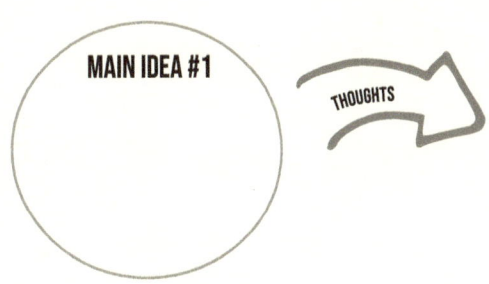

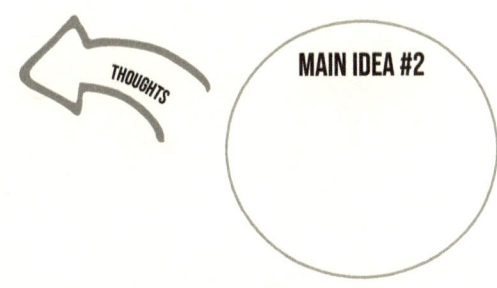

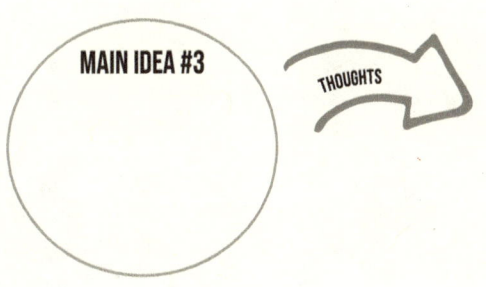

How am I going to apply this to my life this week?

End of the week reflection.
Did I actually apply the message? What was the impact on myself and others?

Alexandria Josey is a native of Charlotte, North Carolina. She is an educator and author of the interactive journal, *Marks of Faith*. Alexandria grew up in the church, and as she grew in her faith, she began to think of a way to make church more meaningful. What started out as a way to stay focused in church, has now turned into an accountability tool for her and others.

She loves to dive deep into the Word and make it relevant to her everyday life. Her friends and peers inspired her to share her notes for others to follow and share. In the interactive journal, *Marks of Faith*, Alexandria provides readers space to mark important takeaways, space to plan how readers will use what they learned, and her favorite part, space to reflect.

www.ingramcontent.com/pod-product-compliance
Lightning Source LLC
Chambersburg PA
CBHW030113240426
43673CB00002B/64